Liqueurs for All Seasons

Liqueurs for All Seasons

Emilio Cocconi

Translated and Adapted by

FRANK KULLA and PATRICIA SHANNON KULLA

Lyceum Books

WILTON, CONNECTICUT

Color photographs by Umberto Marzani.
Special drawings by Marilyn Miller.

First published as *Liquori Casalinghi*
by Fratelli Fabbri Editori, Milan, Italy.

Italian edition © 1974, Fratelli Fabbri
Editori, Milan.
U. S. edition © 1975, Lyceum Books, Inc.,
Wilton, Conn., U. S. A.

Library of Congress Catalog Card Number: 75-26065

Table of Contents

List of Color Photographs   7

About Liqueurs   9

Making Liqueurs   11

Liqueurs for All Seasons — Recipes   13

A Calendar of Liqueurs   117

Index of Liqueur Recipes   121

List of Color Photographs

Aromatic Bitters 17

Banana Liqueur 18

Cream Marsala Liqueur 35

English Walnut Liqueur 36

English Walnut Vermouth 53

Green Tomato Liqueur 54

Hibiscus and Camomile Liqueur; Apple-Tea Liqueur 71

European Mountain Ash Liqueur 72

Lemon Verbena Liqueur 89

Tangerine and Lemon Verbena Liqueur 90

Oranges in Liqueur 107

Wild Plum Liqueur 108

About Liqueurs

The next time you sit down to enjoy a soothing after-dinner liqueur or cup your hand beneath the bowl of a snifter of brandy, consider that the pleasure that comes of all this was once something of a secondary matter. In earlier times, brandies, liqueurs, nearly all spirits of this kind were regarded primarily as medicinal preparations, intended to improve the health of the drinkers.

Until the end of the Middle Ages, wine was the most favored and readily available antiseptic for wounds — it was also drunk for pleasure, of course — and preparations combining certain plants, roots, spices and herbs served as the principal remedies for ailments and diseases. Monks, whose monastery gardens provided the raw materials, were the principal experimenters and concocted most of the early remedies.

In the thirteenth century, Arnau de Vilanova, a chemist and physician from the Catalonia region of Spain, discovered that the essence of herbs, plants and roots could be extracted by steeping them in alcohol for periods of time. The end product was the forerunner of modern liqueurs and the process he used has been employed ever since in producing liqueurs, the process called maceration.

Vilanova and his associate, Raimundo Lulio, were the first to record recipes for liqueurs and to discuss the healing or healthful benefits associated with their use. They were the first to use sweetening to make the liqueurs more palatable, and the first to introduce flavorings that were at the same time healthful — lemon, orange, orange blossom and rose, for example. The Spanish Inquisition, as might be expected, took a dim view of de Vilanova's ideas and he might well have met the executioner but for the intercession of the Pope, whose life he had saved with one of his "pleasant medicines" — a combination of wine, herbs and minute particles of gold.

When the Great Plague swept Europe claiming one-fourth of its population, preparations based on the liqueurs de Vilanova had originated were among the most treasured and sought after medicines. Again, the monasteries were most active in experimenting with these liqueurs. Recipes the monks evolved have been passed down to the present, most of them carefully guarded, and the proprietary liqueurs they produced rank among the best-known in the world — Benedictine and Chartreuse, to name just two.

By the fifteenth century it was generally acknowledged that the Italians were Europe's most accomplished makers of liqueurs. Not only did Catherine de Medici bring a number of the best Italian chefs with her when she came to the French court as the wife of King Henry II, she also brought along a number of her country's best liqueur recipes.

The recipes in this book are not the same as those Catherine carried with her, but they are not all that different. Their origins are identical, although the passage of the centuries has rendered certain ingredients obsolete and certain procedures impractical or unnecessary. Many are recipes that have provided the base formulas for today's most popular commercially-made liqueurs. All are recipes that families not just in Italy but in many other European countries have used for years, and are still using. They rely upon the bounty of the seasons for their flavors and special qualities, and assure a continuous supply of delicious liqueurs throughout all the months of the year — *Liqueurs for All Seasons.*

Making Liqueurs

Where liqueurs are concerned, possibly the only thing easier than making them is drinking them. They require no special equipment, no great mixologist's skill or culinary talent — only good quality ingredients and a bit of patience.

All the liqueurs in this book are made by the time-honored and virtually foolproof process known as maceration. This involves steeping various ingredients — fruits, fruit peel, seeds, nuts, flowers, herbs, spices, leaves, roots — in a spirit base for a specified period of time. The spirit base extracts and absorbs the flavor of the ingredients being macerated. Sometimes the maceration is exposed to the sun to help the absorption. Sweeteners — sugar, syrup, honey, sweetened or fortified wines — are also added for palatability. *None of the liqueurs uses extracts or artificial flavorings.* After the maceration period, the liqueurs are filtered until clear, bottled and set aside to mature and mellow before serving.

Most if not all of the equipment required for making these liqueurs can be found in any home kitchen. The items include: a scale; liquid and dry measures (cups, spoons, etc.); air-tight glass jars of various sizes, such as canning jars or refrigerator jars; a colander or strainer; cheesecloth; filter paper (coffee filters are excellent); a funnel; empty wine or liquor bottles; corks; wax or paraffin for sealing.

The spirit base called for in many of the recipes is 95° alcohol. Pure grain alcohol is not only the best but also the least expensive. It is generally sold as 190° alcohol and should be diluted with an equal quantity of distilled water to achieve the desired 95°. In areas where pure grain alcohol cannot be sold, 80°-100° vodka may be used as a substitute. For best results, the water called for in the recipes should always be distilled water.

Whenever possible, it is best to use fresh ingredients — particularly fresh fruits and vegetables. Dried herbs and spices are, of course, quite acceptable. Some of the herbs called for in the recipes are a bit unusual, but all are available at better herb shops, gourmet and health food stores. There are also a number of shops that offer a broad selection of herbs and spices by mail order.

As to measurements, the U. S. system of measures is often troublesome because of the confusion between liquid and dry measure. Sixteen ounces or two cups dry measure of strawberries, for example, is a considerably different quantity from sixteen ounces or one pound of strawberries by weight. To eliminate such confusion in these recipes, we have used the term ounces for dry ingredients only when they are the same quantity by weight or dry measure. Eight ounces or one cup of sugar dry measure is the equivalent of eight ounces of sugar by weight.

While careful measurement is important, it is really not all that critical. You will find as you make certain liqueurs that you may prefer them less sweet or perhaps more strongly flavored. Simply adjust the ingredients to suit your own taste the next time you make the recipe.

What is important, and may seem curious at first, is the manner in which ingredients are combined and the length of time they are left to macerate. These procedures are the result of years, perhaps even centuries, of trial and error and should be followed carefully.

Certain liqueurs are difficult to filter to absolute clarity, particularly those that are too heavy and syrupy to filter through paper. In these instances, increasing layers or thicknesses of cheesecloth might prove helpful. But if the liqueur remains cloudy, simply cork and set it aside to stand quietly. The residue will settle or hold in suspension after a few months, making it possible to decant the clarified liqueur with little or no difficulty.

One final word, it is also important to let the liqueurs rest and mature for the specified periods before they are served. Taste them after maceration, before bottling, and the taste may seem a bit raw or unfinished. This will disappear, the taste will soften and the bouquet intensify as the liqueur matures.

Liqueurs for All Seasons

Absinthe
Assenziolo

Once thought to affect the brain, absinthe is rarely made today, or it is made with anise as a substitute for the wormwood that was the original base. This recipe is the classic old formula and produces a sharp-tasting, somewhat bitter liqueur of about 40° alcohol that can be a stimulating digestive after a fine dinner.

Ingredients

wormwood	2/3 cup, a mixture of leaves and tops of flowers
calamus	a pinch of the crushed root
cinnamon stick	a pinch
nutmeg, grated	a pinch
cloves	4 whole
coriander	a pinch of seeds
caraway	a pinch of seeds
lemon	sliced peel of one whole lemon (only the yellow)
alcohol 95°	12 ounces
sugar	12 ounces
water	10 ounces
sweet red vermouth	4 ounces

Preparation

Combine the wormwood, calamus, cinnamon, nutmeg, cloves, coriander, caraway and lemon peel together with the alcohol and the vermouth in an air-tight glass jar and allow the ingredients to macerate for three days. Then, dissolve the sugar in the boiled water, let the syrup cool and add it to the contents of the jar. Mix well and let stand for four more days. At the end of this time, strain the mixture through filter paper, funnel the clear liqueur into a dark-glass bottle, cork and seal with wax. Set aside in a cool, dark place to mature for eight months before serving. Makes about 26 ounces.

Almond
Mandorlat

This sweet, rich liqueur is made with a base of almond milk. The aroma is light and delicate, almond faintly touched with spices, and the alcoholic content is relatively low, only 30° to 34° at most.

Ingredients

almond milk	16 ounces
lemon	sliced peel of a half lemon (only the yellow)
cloves	4 whole
cinnamon stick	1/2-inch piece
caraway	a pinch of seeds
sugar	10 ounces
water	10 ounces
alcohol 95°	10 ounces

Preparation

Place the lemon, cloves, cinnamon, caraway and alcohol in an air-tight glass jar and macerate for five days. Then, dissolve the sugar in the boiled water, let the syrup cool and add it to the contents of the jar. Mix well, let stand for two more days, then add the almond milk. Almond milk can be purchased commercially or can be prepared by pounding six ounces of blanched almonds in a mortar or finely shredding them in a blender, combining this with six ounces of sugar, and blending in twelve ounces of distilled water. Shake the mixture well until the sugar is fully absorbed. Mix the almond milk thoroughly with the other ingredients and let the mixture stand for 15 days in a cool, dark place. After this period, filter through several thicknesses of cheesecloth into a dark-glass bottle and cork. Set aside for one or two months before serving. Another filtration may be necessary at this time to remove the additional sediment or residue. Makes about 22 ounces.

Apple

Mele Sciroppate

This is a delightful liqueur and is best made with sharp, crisp, slightly tart eating apples. It has an extremely pleasant taste and a low alcoholic content, about 22°. It can be drunk as a liqueur, served as a syrup over ice cream or cake, and is also delicious diluted with a bit of water and served "on the rocks".

Ingredients:

apples	3 medium, about 1 pound after coring
sugar	16 ounces
lemon	sliced peel of one whole lemon (only the yellow)
rose	10 petals
cloves	2 whole
alcohol 95°	6 ounces

Preparation:

Wash the apples and dry them well. Core and seed them and cut them into convenient pieces, but do not remove the skin. Place the apple pieces in an air-tight clear glass jar with all the other ingredients. Close the top, set the jar in the sun and do not open it until all the sugar has been dissolved and absorbed. Then, strain the liqueur through cheesecloth into a dark-glass bottle and cork. The apples from the maceration may be eaten separately if you desire. Set the liqueur aside in a cool, dark place to mature for two months before serving. Makes about 20 ounces.

Apple-Tea

Kartilla

This liqueur has the appearance and alcoholic content of a brandy, about 40°, but its taste is uniquely its own. The combination of soothing herbal teas, apple and alcohol makes for a liqueur with a lovely bouquet as well as excellent tonic and digestive qualities.

Ingredients:

tea	1 teaspoon of leaves
camomile	1 teaspoon of blossoms
hibiscus	1 teaspoon of petals
apple	1 whole, quartered
lemon	a half, quartered
alcohol 95°	14 ounces
water	16 ounces
sugar	12 ounces

Preparation:

Make an infusion of the tea, camomile and hibiscus, steeping them for six minutes in half of the boiled water. Dissolve the sugar in the other half of the boiled water, let this syrup cool and combine with the infusion, apple, lemon and alcohol in an air-tight glass jar. Close the jar and macerate for 15 days, shaking the jar from time to time to help mix the ingredients. At the end of this period, filter through several thicknesses of cheesecloth into a dark-glass bottle, cork and seal with wax. Set aside to mature in a cool, dark place for at least five months before serving. Makes about 32 ounces.

Apples in Liqueur
Mele Sotto Spirito

Tasty pieces of apple steeped in a lightly
spiced liqueur — served together the combination makes
for a delicious dessert. The liqueur, with an
alcoholic content of about 38°, can also be served
separately and is a fine after-dinner cordial.

Ingredients:

apples	5 medium
cloves	6 whole
cinnamon stick	1/2-inch piece
lemon verbena	2 leaves
sugar	8 ounces
alcohol 95°	14 ounces

Preparation:

Cut the apple into large pieces without peel-
ing and remove the seeds. Macerate with all
of the sugar and four ounces of the alcohol
in an air-tight clear glass jar set in the sun for
one week. Then, add the cloves, cinnamon,
lemon verbena and the rest of the alcohol.
Mix lightly, and let it mature quietly in a cool
dark place for seven months before serving.
Makes about 28 ounces.

Apricot

Albicoc

A popular fruit liqueur, this has a tangy flavor made with dried apricots and a milder, more delicate flavor made with fresh apricots. In either case, the alcoholic content is about 40°.

Ingredients:

apricots	16 ounces fresh or 8 ounces dried
almonds	5 whole (if dried apricots are used)
sugar	10 ounces
cinnamon stick	1/2-inch piece
alcohol 95°	14 ounces

Preparation:

For fresh apricots: pit the fruit and remove the seeds from the pits. Crush the seeds, mix with the apricot pulp and place in an air-tight glass jar to macerate with the other ingredients. For dried apricots: cover with warm water for a few hours to plump. Crush the almonds, add to the drained, plumped apricots and place in an air-tight glass jar to macerate with the other ingredients. In either case, let the maceration stand for three weeks, stirring occasionally. Then, strain through filter paper into a dark-glass bottle, cork and seal with wax. Let it mature quietly for seven months before serving. Makes about 24 ounces.

Arbutus in Liqueur
Corbezzoli Sotto Spirito

A rare and novel liqueur with about 44° alcohol, this tends to have a wonderfully soothing quality, particularly after a large dinner. The fruit steeped in the liqueur is rich and sweet.

Ingredients:

arbutus	16 ounces of berries
lemon	sliced peel of one whole lemon (only the yellow)
lemon verbena	4 leaves
cloves	4 whole
sugar	8 ounces
alcohol 95°	14 ounces

Preparation:

Cut the lemon peel and lemon verbena leaves into thin strips and macerate with all of the other ingredients in an air-tight glass jar for six months. Shake the mixture twice a day for the first two weeks. Then, allow it to mature quietly for the remaining time before serving. Makes about 25 ounces.

Aromatic Bitters

Amarom

This is a dry aromatic bitter liqueur, about 37°
alcohol, with a base of various herbs. It is
stimulating and delicious served as an aperitif and
is also a fine digestive after a full dinner.

Ingredients:

peppermint	5 leaves
pennyroyal	5 leaves
wormwood	10 leaves
sage	5 leaves
lemon verbena	3 leaves
camomile	11 flowers
cinnamon stick	1/2-inch piece
cloves	5 whole
nutmeg, grated	a pinch
anise	1/2 tablespoon of seeds
hibiscus	a tablespoon of petals
lemon	sliced peel of one whole lemon
grapefruit	sliced peel of 1/4 grapefruit (only the yellow)
dandelion	one root, minced
dry white vermouth	22 ounces
alcohol 95°	8 ounces

Preparation:

Macerate all the herbs with the alcohol in an
air-tight glass jar for five days. Strain the
alcohol into a bottle and close. Leave the
residue to macerate with the vermouth in
the air-tight glass jar for another five days.
Strain the vermouth maceration into the
bottle with the strained alcohol. Mix well,
cork, allow to rest for a day, then strain
through filter paper into a dark-glass bottle.
Cork, seal with wax, and let it mature quietly
for at least eight months before serving.
Makes about 32 ounces.

Artichoke
Carciofio

A liqueur with a relatively low alcoholic content, about 30°, made with a base of artichoke leaves, spices and herbs. It can serve both as a tasty aperitif and as a satisfying after-dinner drink.

Ingredients:

artichoke	20 leaves
cloves	2 whole
cinnamon stick	a pinch
sage	1 leaf
basil	1 leaf
caraway	a teaspoon of seeds
coriander	4 seeds
lemon	sliced peel of one whole lemon (only the yellow)
sweet red vermouth	26 ounces
alcohol 95°	6 ounces

Preparation:

Mix the vermouth and alcohol together in an air-tight glass jar with the artichoke leaves and let stand for two days. Strain, put the liquid back into the jar, add all the rest of the ingredients and allow to macerate for one week. Pour through filter paper into a dark-glass bottle, cork, seal with wax and let it mature quietly in a cool dark place for three months before serving. Makes about 28 ounces.

Artichoke and Brandy
Carciofobrandy

This liqueur combines artichoke leaves, white wine and brandy and has an alcoholic content of only 26°. It has a pleasant bouquet and is generally served with a twist of lemon peel as an aperitif.

Ingredients:

artichoke	20 leaves
cloves	2 whole
dry white wine	15 ounces
brandy	14 ounces

Preparation:

Macerate the artichoke leaves, cloves and brandy together in an air-tight glass jar for two days. Add the wine, shake well and let the mixture macerate for another two days. Strain through filter paper into a dark-glass bottle, cork, seal with wax and let it mature quietly for about four months before serving. Makes about 28 ounces.

Banana

Bananio

This is a rich, sweet liqueur with a relatively high alcoholic content of 42°. It is excellent served by itself as a cordial or used as a sauce over ice cream or a macedoine of fruits.

Ingredients:

bananas	about 5 medium-sized
cloves	3 whole
cinnamon stick	a small piece
sweet red vermouth	8 ounces
sugar	20 ounces
alcohol 95°	16 ounces

Preparation:

Peel the bananas, cut them into 1/2-inch slices and place them in an air-tight glass jar with the sugar and vermouth. After ten days, add the other ingredients, mix well and macerate in a cool, dark place for one month. Strain through cheesecloth until clear, funnel into a dark-glass bottle, cork and let it mature quietly for two to three months before serving. Makes about 36 ounces.

Bay Leaf
Laurio

This liqueur is made with a base of bay leaves and has an alcoholic content of about 39°. Its bouquet is pleasant and it is particularly appropriate and delicious served after a fine dinner.

Ingredients:

bay leaves	30 whole
sugar	14 ounces
water	14 ounces
alcohol 95°	16 ounces

Preparation:

Stir the sugar into the water and bring to a boil. Cool the syrup and place in an air-tight glass jar with all the other ingredients for one month, shaking from time to time. After the month's maceration, strain, pass through filter paper into a dark-glass bottle, cork and seal with wax. Let it mature quietly for four months before serving. Makes about 32 ounces.

Blackberries in Liqueur
More Sotto Spirito

Fresh ripe blackberries steeped in a lightly spiced liqueur make for a fine-tasting after-dinner digestive with an alcoholic content of about 41°. The fruit can be used separately to garnish desserts.

Ingredients:

blackberries	1 pound
sugar	14 ounces
alcohol 95°	12 ounces
cloves	6 whole
cinnamon stick	1/2-inch piece
lemon	sliced peel of one whole lemon (only the yellow)

Preparation:

Wash the blackberries carefully and dry them quickly in the sun. Place the blackberries, sugar and half of the alcohol in an air-tight clear glass jar and set it in the sun until all of the sugar is absorbed and dissolved. Then, add the cloves, cinnamon, lemon peel and the rest of the alcohol. Close the jar once again and set it aside in a cool dark place, shaking it gently a few times during the first week. Let it mature quietly for seven months before serving. Makes about 28 ounces.

Blackberry Brandy
Rov - Brandy

A combination of dry brandy and sweet ripe blackberries produces a liqueur with a relatively low alcoholic content, about 31°, and excellent tonic qualities that can be served almost any time of the day.

Ingredients:

dry brandy	20 ounces
blackberries	10 ounces

Preparation:

Crush the blackberries and put them into an air-tight glass jar with the brandy to macerate for 20 days. Shake the jar twice a day during the first week. After the maceration period, strain, pass through filter paper into a dark-glass bottle, close and seal with wax. Let it mature quietly for eight months before serving. Makes about 24 ounces.

Black Currant
Gribes

An aromatic fruit brandy made with black currants,
this has a delightfully robust taste and an
alcoholic content of about 38°. It is served exclusively
as a liqueur, with or without the currants.

Ingredients:

brandy	24 ounces
black currants	2 ounces

Preparation:

Place the black currants and brandy in a dark-glass bottle. Cork, seal with wax, and let it mature quietly in a cool dark place for ten months before serving. Makes about 25 ounces.

Camomile
Camilla

Made with a base of camomile flowers, this liqueur is a mild and soothing digestive, especially welcome in the evening after a large dinner. About 40° alcohol, it can be served warm or cool.

Ingredients:

camomile	1½ cup of flowers
lemon	sliced peel of one whole lemon (only the yellow) and the pulp of ¼ lemon
carrot	a pinch of seeds
sugar	12 ounces
water	12 ounces
alcohol	12 ounces

Preparation:

Place the camomile flowers, lemon peel, lemon pulp and alcohol in an air-tight glass jar and macerate for two weeks. Then, dissolve the sugar in the boiled water, let the syrup cool and add it to the contents of the jar. Close the jar again, shake well and allow to stand for four weeks. Filter through cheesecloth into a dark-glass bottle, cork and let it mature quietly for at least three months before serving. Makes about 26 ounces.

Caraway
Carvel

This aromatic liqueur has a base of caraway, about 40° alcohol, and characteristics similar to kummel and akvavit. It has both stimulative and digestive qualities and can be served before or after dinner.

Ingredients:

caraway	2 tablespoons of seeds
cloves	4 whole
anise	a teaspoon of seeds
coriander	½ teaspoon of seeds
sugar	18 ounces
water	14 ounces
alcohol 95°	16 ounces

Preparation:

Macerate all of the ingredients except the sugar and water in an air-tight glass jar for two weeks. Then, dissolve the sugar in the boiled water, cool and add the syrup to the jar. Mix well and let stand for two more weeks. Strain through filter paper into a dark-glass bottle, cork and seal with wax. Let it mature quietly for eight months before serving. Makes about 36 ounces.

Carnation, Wild
Garofanolo

An unusual liqueur with a base of wild carnations and an
alcoholic content about 41°. It has a fine flavor,
a clove-like aroma typical of the flowers, and can be
served as a tonic or as an after-dinner cordial.

Ingredients:

wild carnation (clove pink)	1¼ cup of petals
sugar	14 ounces
lemon	sliced peel of a half lemon (only the yellow)
water	8 ounces
alcohol 95°	10 ounces
brandy	4 ounces

Preparation:

Blend the petals well with the sugar, beating
for a few minutes perhaps with a little of the
alcohol. Place in an air-tight glass jar with the
rest of the alcohol, close tightly and let the
mixture stand for ten days, shaking from
time to time. Then, dissolve the sugar in the
boiled water, cool and add this syrup to the
jar. Close, shake well and let stand for one
week. Strain and pass through filter paper
into a dark-glass bottle. Cork, seal with wax
and let it mature quietly for three to five
months before serving. Makes about 22
ounces.

Cherry
Ciliegie Liquorose

This liqueur has a base of whole cherries and an alcoholic content of 18°. An excellent digestive at the end of a meal, it is also refreshing at any time diluted with a splash of water and served "on the rocks".

Ingredients:

sweet cherries	1½ pounds
lemon	sliced peel of a half lemon (only the yellow)
sugar	28 ounces
dry white vermouth	28 ounces

Preparation:

Pull the stems off half the cherries and cut off the other stems near the fruit. Place the cherries, lemon peel (cut into thin strips), sugar and vermouth in an air-tight glass jar and macerate for one month, shaking gently from time to time. At the end of this period, strain, pass through filter paper into a dark-glass bottle, cork and set aside in a cool, dark place. Let it mature quietly for six months before serving. Makes about 1½ quarts.

Cherry, Black
Maresco

Made with crushed sweet black cherries, this liqueur
has an alcoholic content of 40° and tonic as
well as digestive qualities. Its delightful taste matches
its appealing deep cherry red color.

Ingredients:

sweet black cherries	2½ cups, pitted
cherry pits	10 crushed
cloves	5 whole
cinnamon stick	½-inch piece
lemon	sliced peel of one whole lemon (only the yellow)
cherry leaves	10 whole
sugar	8 ounces
alcohol 95°	14 ounces

Preparation:

Crush the pitted cherries and macerate the
pulp, about ten of the crushed pits and all of
the other ingredients for one week in an air-
tight glass jar exposed to the sun, shaking
from time to time. Then, place it in a cool
dark place to macerate five weeks longer.
Strain through cheesecloth and filter paper
until clear, funnel into a dark-glass bottle,
cork and seal with wax. Let it mature quietly
for eight months before serving. Makes
about 26 ounces.

Cherry Leaf
Marenbianc

A pale yellow liqueur, about 38° alcohol, made from the leaves of the black cherry tree. It is particularly delicious as an after-dinner cordial and may also be served with certain desserts.

Ingredients:

black cherry	75 leaves
lemon	sliced peel of a half lemon (only the yellow)
sweet white wine	26 ounces
sugar	4 ounces
alcohol 95°	10 ounces

Preparation:

Macerate the cherry leaves, sugar, wine and lemon peel in an air-tight glass jar for 45 days, shaking it from time to time. Then, add the alcohol, close tightly once again, shake well and let it stand for 20 more days. Strain, pass through filter paper into a dark-glass bottle, cork and seal with wax. Let it mature quietly for six months before serving. Makes about 36 ounces.

Cherry Leaf, Semi-Dry

Marenross

A semi-dry red liqueur made from the leaves of the black cherry tree. With an alcoholic content of 35°, it is especially welcome as a digestive after dinner.

Ingredients:

black cherry	80 leaves
lemon	sliced peel of a half lemon (only the yellow)
sparkling red wine, semi-dry	25 ounces
sugar	6 ounces
alcohol 95°	10 ounces

Preparation:

Macerate the cherry leaves, sugar, wine and lemon peel in an air-tight glass jar for 45 days, shaking it from time to time. Then, add the alcohol, mix well and let it stand for another 20 days. After this period, strain, pass through filter paper into a dark-glass bottle, cork and seal with wax. Let it mature quietly for six months before serving. Makes about 34 ounces.

Cherry, Morello or Tart
Marescato

This is a tart cherry liqueur made with morello cherries. About 44° alcohol, it has both tonic and digestive qualities and a full, rich cherry taste.

Ingredients:

large morello cherries	1 pound
cloves	5 whole
cinnamon stick	½-inch piece
peppermint	2 leaves
sugar	4 ounces
alcohol 95°	12 ounces

Preparation:

Wash, dry and stem the cherries very carefully. Let them macerate with the sugar in a clear glass jar with the top open in the sun for one day. Add all of the other ingredients and close the jar, making it airtight. Agitate very delicately twice a day for one week. Then, place the jar in a cool dark place to mature quietly for eight months before serving. Makes about 22 ounces.

Cherry, Sweet
Ciliegiolo

A sweet cherry liqueur with an alcoholic content of
about 40°. It is an excellent digestive after
a full meal and can also be served with certain desserts.

Ingredients:

sweet black cherries	1 pound
sugar	8 ounces
water	4 ounces
alcohol 95°	12 ounces

Preparation:

Pound the cherries with their pits in a mortar and let this pulp sit, covered, in a dark place for 20 hours. Strain through cheesecloth to extract the juice. Bring the water to a boil and dissolve the sugar in it. Cool and add this syrup to the cherry juice. Place all the ingredients in an air-tight glass jar, mix well, and let it stand for one week. Then, strain through filter paper into a dark-glass bottle and cork. Let it mature quietly for six months before serving. Makes about one quart.

Coconut
Zoccolino

A dry liqueur with a base of fresh coconut and brandy. About 40° alcohol, its bouquet is touched with the sweet fragrance of the coconut. It can be served at any time of day, but is best after dinner as a digestive.

Ingredients:

fresh coconut	16 ounces of the white flesh
coriander	5 seeds
juniper	5 berries
brandy	20 ounces
alcohol 95°	4 ounces

Preparation:

Cut the coconut into little pieces and macerate them in an air-tight glass jar with the coriander, juniper berries, brandy and alcohol for three weeks. Keep the jar sheltered from the light and shake it delicately from time to time. After the maceration period, strain through filter paper into a dark-glass bottle and cork. Let it mature quietly for four months before serving. Makes about 24 ounces.

Coffee
Brasilio

One of the most popular of all liqueurs, this
is made with a base of double-roasted espresso coffee.
It has an alcoholic content of about 40° and
is probably best served as a digestive after dinner.

Ingredients:

coffee	5 ounces of strong, freshly made espresso
vanilla	a pinch of crushed bean
lemon	sliced peel of one whole lemon (only the yellow)
sugar	14 ounces
water	14 ounces
alcohol 95°	14 ounces

Preparation:

Macerate the coffee, the lemon peel cut into thin strips, and the vanilla in an airtight glass jar for one week. Then, bring the water to a boil and dissolve the sugar in it. Cool and add the syrup to the contents of the jar, along with the alcohol. Let it stand for another week, stirring once a day. At the end of this time, strain through filter paper into a dark-glass bottle and cork. Let it mature quietly for two months before serving. Makes about 34 ounces.

Cream Marsala
L'Ovet

A creamy rich liqueur that combines milk, eggs and marsala wine. It has an alcoholic content of 20° and a taste reminiscent of the classic Italian dessert, zabaglione. It can be served as a liqueur but is particularly delicious when served as a sauce over ice cream or cake.

Ingredients:

eggs	5 yolks
milk	8 ounces
sugar	12 ounces
dry marsala wine	8 ounces
vanilla	a small piece of the bean
alcohol 95°	6 ounces

Preparation:

Combine the egg yolks and sugar in the top of a glass double boiler or enamel pan. Slowly add the milk, half of the marsala and the vanilla, blending with a whisk to avoid lumps. Bring the mixture to a boil and simmer for five minutes. Watch it carefully so that it does not scorch and continue to stir it throughout this time with the whisk or a wooden spoon. Remove it from the heat, cool to lukewarm — still stirring — and add the rest of the marsala and the alcohol. Take out the vanilla bean, pour the liqueur into a bottle or air-tight jar and close tightly. Shake it well and let it mature for two months before serving. If the jar is left tightly closed in a cool dark place, the liqueur will keep indefinitely, since the alcohol acts as a preservative. Makes about 28 ounces.

Eggnog
Iovo

A sweet dessert liqueur with a base of eggs and milk
and a low alcoholic content, only 18° at most.
It is rich and nutritious and is often recommended as
a tonic to be served to convalescents.

Ingredients:

milk	16 ounces
eggs	5 yolks
sugar	16 ounces
vanilla	a small piece of the bean
dry marsala wine	10 ounces
alcohol 95°	6 ounces

Preparation:

Bring the milk to a boil with the vanilla bean, remove from the heat and stir in half of the sugar until dissolved. Cool. Blend the egg yolks into the rest of the sugar and, little by little, add the marsala and the alcohol, beating well with a whisk. Remove the vanilla bean from the cooled milk and slowly add the milk to the other mixture, beating all the while with the whisk. Continue beating a few minutes longer after all the ingredients have been combined. Then, strain the liqueur through a colander into a dark-glass bottle, cork tightly and set aside to mature quietly for two months before serving. If the bottle is left tightly closed in a cool dark place, the liqueur will keep indefinitely, since the alcohol acts as a preservative. Makes about 34 ounces.

Elderberries, Huckleberries or Bilberries in Liqueur

Mirtilli Sotto Spirito

Tart berries steeped in a mixture of sweet white wine and natural spirits create an inviting rose-colored liqueur of 38° alcohol. It is especially appropriate after dinner, served with or without the berries.

Ingredients:

elderberries, huckleberries or bilberries	3½ cups
cloves	3 whole
lemon verbena	3 leaves
lemon	sliced peel of ½ lemon
tarragon	a pinch
alcohol 95°	10 ounces
sweet white wine	8 ounces

Preparation:

Combine all of the ingredients in an air-tight glass jar and macerate for five months. The berries may be served with the liqueur if you desire, or the fruit and lemon peel may be strained off before serving. Makes about 22 ounces.

Elderberry, Huckleberry or Bilberry

Mirtillino

Less than 14° alcohol, this liqueur makes an excellent dessert syrup and may also be used as a substitute for grenadine. Served over ice with a splash of water or soda, it is a delightfully thirst-quenching drink.

Ingredients:

elderberries, huckleberries or bilberries	2 cups
sugar	16 ounces
lemon	sliced peel of ¼ lemon (only the yellow)
alcohol 95°	4 ounces
semi-sweet white wine	4 ounces

Preparation:

Combine all of the ingredients in an air-tight glass jar and macerate in the sun for one month, shaking frequently. After this time, let it mature quietly in a cool dark place for four months. Strain off the fruit and lemon peel before serving. Makes about 24 ounces.

Elderberry, Huckleberry or Bilberry, Sweet

Mirtecco

This sweet fruit liqueur, about 38° alcohol, is delicious
any time, but especially after a large dinner. It
can also be served mixed into whipped cream or ice cream
and is an excellent complement to many desserts.

Ingredients:

elderberries, huckleberries or bilberries	4 cups
sugar	16 ounces
lemon	sliced peel of ¼ lemon
alcohol 95°	16 ounces

Preparation:

Pour the berries into an air-tight glass jar.
Add the sugar, the lemon peel cut into thin
strips, and cover with the alcohol. Close the
jar tightly and macerate in the sun for one
month, shaking frequently. Then, transfer
the jar to a cool dark place and let the liqueur mature quietly for another five
months. Strain through filter paper after this
time into a dark-glass bottle and cork.
Makes about 36 ounces.

English Walnut
Nocino Normale

A rather strong liqueur, alcoholic content about 50°, made with a base of English walnuts. It is a remarkably good digestive and is particularly welcome served at the end of a fine, full dinner.

Ingredients:

English walnuts	20 whole
cloves	15 whole
cinnamon stick	1-inch piece
lemon	sliced peel of 1 whole lemon
sugar	14 ounces
sweet sparkling white wine	16 ounces
alcohol 95°	34 ounces

Preparation:

The original recipe for this liqueur uses green English walnuts, including the outer hull. When walnuts are green or unripe, they can be easily sliced. Cut ten of the green walnuts in half and the rest in quarters. If only dried English walnuts are available — the kind sold commercially — use just the nut meats and not the shells. The taste will be somewhat different, but still quite good. Place the nuts, cloves, vanilla, the lemon peel cut into thin strips, and the alcohol in an air-tight glass jar and macerate for five weeks, shaking the jar occasionally to help mix the ingredients. At the end of this time, strain through a colander and return to the jar. (The residue in the colander can be used to make English Walnut Vermouth.) Dissolve the sugar in the wine, add this to the jar, close tightly and let it stand for six months. Funnel through filter paper into a dark-glass bottle, cork, seal with wax, and allow to mature for one more month before serving. Makes about 50 ounces.

English Walnut Brandy

Nocino Super

A dry liqueur with a base of English walnuts and brandy and an alcoholic content about 54°. It has a robust flavor, excellent tonic and digestive qualities, and makes an interesting substitute for after-dinner cognac.

Ingredients:

English walnuts	12 whole
cloves	8 whole
cinnamon stick	1-inch piece
lemon	sliced peel of 2 whole lemons
thyme	a pinch
peppermint	2 leaves
lemon verbena	2 leaves
sage	2 leaves
basil	2 leaves
sugar	6 ounces
brandy	16 ounces
alcohol 95°	16 ounces
sweet madeira wine	8 ounces

Preparation:

The original recipe for this liqueur calls for green or unripe English walnuts and utilizes the entire nut, including the outer hull which can be cut through easily when it is green. Cut six of the nuts in half and the rest in quarters. If only dried English walnuts are available — the kind sold commercially — use just the nut meats and not the shells. The taste will be somewhat different, but still quite good. Place all of the ingredients in an air-tight glass jar and macerate them for 40 days, shaking the jar from time to time. After this period, strain through a colander and then through filter paper into a dark-glass bottle. (The residue in the colander can be used to make English Walnut Vermouth.) Cork the bottle, seal with wax, and let the liqueur mature quietly for eight months before serving. Makes about 38 ounces.

English Walnut, Dry

Nocino Secco

A liqueur with a base of English walnuts and madeira wine. This is another robust walnut liqueur, about 43° alcohol, that can be appreciated after dinner both for its fine bouquet and for its tonic-digestive qualities.

Ingredients:

English walnuts	11 whole
cloves	8 whole
cinnamon stick	1-inch piece
lemon	sliced peel of 1 whole lemon
caraway	1 tablespoon seeds
sugar	4 ounces
sweet madeira wine	16 ounces
alcohol 95°	10 ounces

Preparation:

The original recipe for this liqueur uses green English walnuts, including the outer hull. When walnuts are green or unripe, they can be easily sliced. Cut five of the green walnuts in half and the rest in quarters. If only dried English walnuts are available — the kind sold commercially — use just the nut meats and not the shells. The taste will be somewhat different, but still quite good. Place the nuts, cloves, cinnamon, lemon peel, caraway and alcohol in an air-tight glass jar and macerate for five weeks, shaking the jar occasionally to help mix the ingredients. Then, strain through a colander and funnel into a dark-glass bottle. (The residue in the colander can be used to make English Walnut Vermouth.) Dissolve the sugar in the wine and add this to the bottle. Cork, seal with wax, shake well and set in a cool dark place for eight months. At the end of this time, filter the liqueur through several thicknesses of cheesecloth and funnel it into a clean dark-glass bottle. Cork, seal with wax once again, and let it mature quietly for another four months before serving. Makes about 32 ounces.

English Walnut Vermouth

Vernoce

An aperitif with a base of English walnuts and vermouth and an alcoholic content around 17°. It has an interesting robust flavor and can serve both as a stimulating tonic and as a digestive.

Ingredients:

strained residue from the preparation of any of the English walnut liqueurs

cloves	4 whole
cinnamon stick	½-inch piece
dry white vermouth	enough to cover all the ingredients

Preparation:

Pour the strained residue into an air-tight glass jar along with the cloves, cinnamon, and enough vermouth to cover all the ingredients. Close the jar tightly, shake it a bit to help mix the ingredients, and set it in the sun for one week. Then, place it in a cool dark place to macerate for five more weeks. After this time, strain through filter paper into a dark-glass bottle, cork and let it mature quietly for another four months before serving.

Four Fruits
Tetrafrutto

A semi-dry liqueur, about 41° alcohol, with a base of four kinds of fruit. This is not only exquisite and delightful as a liqueur, but is also refreshing served over ice with a twist of lemon peel.

Ingredients:

strawberries	¼ pint
elderberries, huckleberries or bilberries	¼ pint
raspberries	¼ pint
gooseberries, ripe	¼ pint
sugar	8 ounces
alcohol 95°	12 ounces

Preparation:

Crush the fruit in a bowl, mix it well with the sugar and place in the refrigerator for three to four hours. Transfer the crushed pulp and all of the liquid into an air-tight glass jar, mix in the alcohol, close and macerate for two weeks. Then, strain through cheesecloth and filter paper into a dark-glass bottle, cork and seal with wax. Let it mature quietly for eight months before serving. Makes about 22 ounces.

Fourteen Herbs
Erba 14

An aromatic herb liqueur with a base of 14 herbs, an alcoholic content of 40°-42°, and a taste similar to yellow chartreuse. This liqueur is not only a fine digestive, but also makes an excellent aperitif.

Ingredients:

lemon	5 leaves
bay leaf	5 whole
cherry	5 whole leaves or a good-sized pinch of cherry bark
pennyroyal	5 leaves
lemon verbena	5 leaves
basil	5 leaves
sage	5 leaves
rosemary	6 leaves or a good-sized pinch of the crushed herb
cloves	5 whole
juniper	5 berries
melissa	5 leaves
camomile	a pinch of flowers
hibiscus	a tablespoon of petals
cinnamon stick	½-inch piece
sugar	12 ounces
water	12 ounces
alcohol 95°	14 ounces

Preparation:

Macerate all of the herbs with the alcohol in an air-tight glass jar for five days. Then, bring the water to a boil and dissolve the sugar in it. Cool the syrup, add it to the jar, mix well, and let it stand three to four days longer. Filter through cheesecloth and filter paper into a dark-glass bottle and cork. After four months, strain again through filter paper, funnel into a clean dark-glass bottle, cork and seal with wax. Let it mature quietly for five or six months before serving. Makes about 26 ounces.

Gooseberry
Ribeso

A liqueur with a base of gooseberries and an alcoholic content about 40°. It has a rich, appetizing red-purple color and a lovely, full fruit flavor.

Ingredients:

gooseberries, ripe	1 pound
sugar	8 ounces
alcohol 95°	12 ounces

Preparation:

Crush the gooseberries and put them into an air-tight glass jar with the sugar and alcohol. Macerate for a few days in the sun until the sugar dissolves completely, shaking gently from time to time. It may be advisable to cover the jar with a thin cloth on extremely bright days so that the exposure to sunlight is not too strong. When the sugar has been fully absorbed and turned to syrup, filter the maceration through cheesecloth and then through filter paper, funnel into a dark-glass bottle and cork. Let it mature quietly for six months before serving. Makes about 24 ounces.

Green Tomato
Tomacchino

A classic and unusual liqueur made with a base of green tomatoes combined with various herbs. The taste is sweet, the alcoholic content about 23°, and the reaction of guests to whom it is served is surprise and delight.

Ingredients:

green tomatoes	1 pound
tomato leaves	4 whole
sage	6 leaves
rosemary	a 3-inch sprig
lemon verbena	6 leaves
lemon or lime	4 leaves
brandy	8 ounces
alcohol 95°	8 ounces
sugar	24 ounces
water	6 ounces

Preparation:

Cut the tomatoes into thin pieces and crush them in a bowl with 16 ounces of the sugar. Transfer the mixture to an air-tight glass jar and add the brandy and all the other ingredients except the alcohol, water and the rest of the sugar. Close the jar and let it stand out of the light for four days, shaking it occasionally to help mix the ingredients. Then, bring the water to a boil and dissolve the rest of the sugar in it. Cool the syrup and add it to the jar along with the alcohol. Close again, shake well to mix, and set in a cool dark place for ten days. At the end of this period, strain through a colander and then through filter paper into a dark-glass bottle. Cork and set aside to mature quietly for three months before serving. Makes about 30 ounces.

Herbs and Brandy

Brandyarom

This liqueur, made with a base of brandy and various aromatic herbs, has a strong bouquet and an alcoholic content of about 40°. It is most frequently served as an after-dinner digestive.

Ingredients:

chicory	a medium root, chopped
bramble or wild rose	40 petals
anise	1 teaspoon seeds
coriander	1 teaspoon seeds
licorice	a pinch of crushed root
wormwood	a pinch
brandy	24 ounces

Preparation:

Macerate all of the ingredients in an air-tight jar for one week. Strain through filter paper into a dark-glass bottle, cork and seal with wax. Let it mature quietly for six months before serving. Makes about 24 ounces.

Hibiscus and Camomile
Karkam

A soothing liqueur, about 41° alcohol, made of camomile and hibiscus blossoms. It has an appealing rose color, a pleasant taste, and is a fine digestive.

Ingredients:

camomile	4 teaspoons of flowers
hibiscus	3 tablespoons of petals
lemon	sliced peel of 1 whole lemon (only the yellow)
melissa	8 leaves
water	20 ounces
alcohol 95°	12 ounces
sugar	8 ounces

Preparation:

Bring the water to a boil and steep the camomile and hibiscus in it for six minutes. Strain this warm infusion and dissolve the sugar in it. Cool and pour into an air-tight glass jar with the melissa, lemon peel and alcohol. Macerate for five weeks, then strain through filter paper into a dark-glass bottle, cork and seal with wax. Let it mature quietly for seven months before serving. Makes about 30 ounces.

Jujubes in Liqueur

Giuggiole Sotto Spirito

Date-like jujubes provide the base for this interesting liqueur. About 42° alcohol, it is sweet, flavorful, and is best served as a digestive.

Ingredients:

jujubes	1 pound
vanilla	a pinch of crushed bean
lemon	sliced peel of ¼ lemon
sugar	8 ounces
alcohol 95°	12 ounces

Preparation:

Place the jujubes, sugar, lemon peel cut into thin strips, vanilla and one-fourth of the alcohol into a clear air-tight glass jar. Close tightly and set the jar in the sun, shaking from time to time, until the sugar is dissolved. Then, add the rest of the alcohol, shake well and put in a cool dark place to mature quietly for six months. It may be served with the fruit or strained and served separately as a liqueur. Makes about 20 ounces.

Juniper
Gineprino

This liqueur, about 40° alcohol, has a base of juniper berries. Its taste is reminiscent of gin, which is also made of junipers, although a bit sweeter.

Ingredients:

juniper	100 berries
sugar	12 ounces
water	12 ounces
alcohol 95°	10 ounces

Preparation:

Macerate the juniper berries with the alcohol in an air-tight glass jar for four weeks. Then, dissolve the sugar in the boiled water and allow the syrup to cool. Strain the juniper berry maceration through filter paper and combine the filtered liqueur with the sugar syrup. Mix well, transfer to a dark-glass bottle, cork and seal with wax. Let it mature quietly for eight months before serving. Makes about 24 ounces.

Lemon and Orange

Limonarancio

A fairly dry liqueur with a base of lemon and orange
peel. About 43° alcohol, it has a pleasantly
citrus bouquet and tonic as well as digestive qualities.

Ingredients:

orange	sliced peel of 4 oranges (only the orange part)
lemon	sliced peel of 4 lemons (only the yellow)
sugar	6 ounces
brandy	32 ounces
sweet sparkling white wine	8 ounces
alcohol 95°	8 ounces

Preparation:

Place the orange and lemon peel into an air-tight glass jar with the sugar, brandy, wine and alcohol and macerate for three months. Then, strain through filter paper into a dark-glass bottle, cork and seal with wax. Let it mature quietly for seven months before serving. Makes about 48 ounces.

Lemon Verbena
Maria Luigia

A delicately sweet liqueur with a base of lemon verbena.
About 36° alcohol, it has an exquisite bouquet
and can serve equally well as an aperitif or digestive.

Ingredients:

lemon verbena	90 leaves
peppermint	4 leaves
basil	2 leaves
lemon	1 large, quartered
sugar	24 ounces
water	24 ounces
alcohol 95°	20 ounces

Preparation:

Dissolve the sugar in the boiled water and cool. Pour the syrup into an air-tight glass jar with all the other ingredients and macerate for one month, shaking from time to time. Then, strain through cheesecloth and filter paper into a dark-glass bottle, cork, seal with wax and let it mature quietly for at least eight months. If it still appears cloudy when ready to serve, strain again through filter paper into a new bottle. Makes about 48 ounces.

Lemon Verbena, Dry

Luigiara

A dry liqueur, about 40° alcohol, with a base of lemon verbena. It has both tonic and digestive qualities and a taste as appealing as its bouquet.

Ingredients:

lemon verbena	25 leaves
lemon	sliced peel of 1 whole lemon (only the yellow)
caraway	a pinch of seeds
peppermint	5 leaves
basil	5 leaves
dry white vermouth	20 ounces
alcohol 95°	8 ounces

Preparation:

Place all the dry ingredients in an air-tight glass jar along with the vermouth and alcohol and macerate for five weeks. Then, strain through filter paper into a dark-glass bottle, cork and seal with wax. Let it mature quietly for eight months before serving. Makes about 26 ounces.

Loquat or Yellow Plum

Nespolio

A pleasant-tasting fruit liqueur made of loquats or,
as a substitute, yellow plums. It has an
alcoholic content of 40° and is best served as a digestive.

Ingredients:

loquats or yellow plums, pitted	¾ pound
vanilla	a pinch of crushed bean
lemon	sliced peel of ½ lemon
sugar	8 ounces
alcohol 95°	10 ounces

Preparation:

Lightly heat the pitted loquats or yellow plums with the sugar just until the sugar dissolves, stirring with a wooden spoon. Remove from the heat, add the vanilla and stir well to cool. Strain through a colander and put the juice obtained into an air-tight glass jar along with the alcohol and the lemon peel cut into thin strips. Shake well to mix and let it stand for one month. Then, strain through filter paper into a dark-glass bottle, cork and let it mature quietly for four months before serving. Makes about 20 ounces.

Loquat or Yellow Plum, Sweet

Nespolino

This is a liqueur made with a base of loquat or, as a substitute, yellow plum seeds and an alcoholic content of about 40°. The taste is soft and delicate, touched with the sweet essence of the fruit.

Ingredients:

loquat or yellow plum seeds	1 cup
vanilla	a pinch of crushed bean
domestic rose	6 petals
melissa	4 leaves
alcohol 95°	12 ounces
water	12 ounces
sugar	12 ounces

Preparation:

Spread the loquat or yellow plum seeds on a sheet of paper to dry in the sun for ten days. If loquats are used, peel the papery covering off the seeds. After the seeds are dry, place them in an air-tight clear glass jar along with the melissa, vanilla, rose petals and alcohol. Bring the water to a boil, dissolve the sugar in it, cool and add this syrup to the jar. Close tightly and let the ingredients macerate in the sun for one month, agitating the jar several times during this period. Then, strain through filter paper into a dark-glass bottle, cork and let it mature quietly for three months before serving. Makes about 26 ounces.

Melissa
Melisso

A soothing herb liqueur, about 40° alcohol, with a base of melissa (lemon balm). An excellent stimulant, tonic and digestive, it is a welcome cordial at almost any time.

Ingredients:

melissa (lemon balm)	45 leaves
lemon	sliced peel of ½ lemon (only the yellow)
carrot	a pinch of seeds
cinnamon stick	½-inch piece
coriander	a pinch of seeds
peppermint	4 leaves
sugar	12 ounces
water	12 ounces
alcohol 95°	12 ounces

Preparation:

Bring the water to a boil, dissolve the sugar in it and remove immediately from the heat. Cool the syrup and pour it into an air-tight glass jar along with all the other ingredients. Close tightly, shake well to mix, and macerate for three weeks, agitating the jar once a day during the maceration period. After this time, strain through a sieve and then through filter paper into a dark-glass bottle. Cork, seal with wax and let it mature quietly for seven months before serving. Makes about 28 ounces.

Milk and Cherries
De Vecchia

A creamy-smooth liqueur with a base of milk
and pitted sweet cherries. It has an alcoholic content
of 38° and is nutritious as well as very tasty.

Ingredients:

milk	20 ounces
sweet cherries, pitted	4 ounces
sugar	20 ounces
lemon	1 whole
vanilla	a pinch of crushed bean
alcohol 95°	20 ounces

Preparation:

Cut half of the lemon into thin slices and use just the peel of the other half (only the yellow) cut into thin strips. Place these, along with all the other ingredients, into an air-tight glass jar and macerate for three weeks, agitating the jar twice each day during the maceration period. At the end of this time, strain through a colander and then through filter paper into dark-glass bottles. Cork, seal with wax and let the liqueur mature quietly for seven months before serving. Makes about 50 ounces.

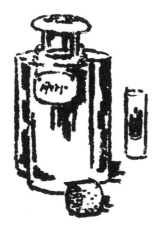

Mixed Mint

Mentamix

A liqueur with a base of peppermint and pennyroyal
and an alcoholic content about 36°. It has a bouquet and
taste reminiscent of creme dementhe and is
particularly refreshing and satisfying after dinner.

Ingredients:

peppermint	15 leaves
pennyroyal	15 leaves
basil	2 leaves
lemon	sliced peel of ½ lemon (only the yellow)
cloves	2 whole
sugar	12 ounces
water	12 ounces
alcohol 95°	10 ounces

Preparation:

If fresh mint leaves are used, gather those closest to the flowers since they are more fragrant. Dissolve the sugar in the water which has been brought to a boil. Remove immediately from the heat, cool, and pour the syrup into an air-tight glass jar along with all the other ingredients. Close tightly and macerate for one month, shaking the jar occasionally. After this period, filter through cheesecloth into a dark-glass bottle, cork, seal with wax and let it mature quietly for eight months. If the liqueur is still cloudy at that time, filter it rapidly through cheesecloth into a new bottle before serving. Makes about 22 ounces.

Hibiscus and Camomile Liqueur; Apple-Tea Liqueur

Mountain Ash, European

Sorbolo

An unusual liqueur made from the edible fruit of the European mountain ash, also known as the rowan tree. It has a delicious taste, an alcoholic content of 41°, and is considered an excellent digestive.

Ingredients:

European mountain ash	1 pound of the fruit
cloves	3 whole
lemon	sliced peel of one whole lemon (only the yellow)
cinnamon stick	½-inch piece
sugar	8 ounces
alcohol 95°	12 ounces

Preparation:

Place all of the ingredients in a clear air-tight glass jar and macerate for six months. Expose the jar to the sun for the first ten days and agitate frequently. Then, set aside in a cool, dark place for the remainder of the time. At the end of the maceration period, strain through filter paper into a dark-glass bottle, cork and allow to mature quietly for four months before serving. Makes about 20 ounces.

Mulberry
Morolo

A sweet fruit liqueur with a base of mulberries.
About 40° alcohol, it has a deep red-purple color and
a delightfully appealing full-fruit taste.

Ingredients:

mulberries	1 pound
sugar	8 ounces
alcohol 95°	14 ounces

Preparation:

Place the berries in a clear air-tight glass jar
with all of the sugar and half of the alcohol
and expose to the sun until the sugar is absorbed. Set the jar in the shade for an hour
or so before adding the rest of the alcohol.
Reclose, expose to the sun for one more
day, then transfer the jar to a cool, dark
place for one month, agitating very
delicately from time to time. At the end of
this period, strain through filter paper into a
dark-glass bottle, cork, seal with wax and
serve after one month. Makes about 24
ounces.

Orange and Lemon
Bucciarancio

A liqueur made from the peel of oranges and lemons, with
an alcoholic content about 39°-40°. It has a rich
golden color and can be served at almost any time of day.

Ingredients:

oranges	sliced peel of 4 oranges (only the orange part)
lemons	sliced peel of 2 lemons (only the yellow)
lime	sliced peel of ½ lime (only the green)
tangerine	1 small, quartered
sugar	12 ounces
water	12 ounces
alcohol 95°	12 ounces

Preparation:

Bring the water to a boil, remove from the heat and dissolve the sugar in it. Cool this syrup and place it in an air-tight glass jar with all of the other ingredients. Close it tightly and macerate for ten days, shaking every now and then. After the maceration period, strain through cheesecloth into a dark-glass bottle, cork and seal with wax. Let it mature quietly for six months before serving. Makes about 26 ounces.

Orange and Pear
Aranper

This liqueur has a base of oranges and pears and an alcoholic content about 30°. It is a sweet, mellow cordial and is also delicious as a dessert sauce.

Ingredients:

oranges	2 medium, peeled
pears	2 medium, peeled and cored
sugar	10 ounces
alcohol 95°	8 ounces

Preparation:

Cut the pears into slices and place them into a clear air-tight glass jar with the sugar. Close tightly and expose to the sun for one week, shaking occasionally to help the sugar dissolve. Then, cut the oranges into wedges and add to the jar along with the alcohol. Mix and let it stand for four weeks, shaking from time to time. At the end of the maceration period, strain through filter paper into a dark-glass bottle and cork. Let it mature quietly for seven months before serving. Makes about 20 ounces.

Orange, Bitter

Bergamot

This liqueur is made with a base of Bergamot or bitter oranges and has an alcoholic content about 36°.
It is richly aromatic and has a pleasantly bitter taste.

Ingredients:

Bergamot (bitter) oranges	½ pound
sugar	12 ounces
water	6 ounces
alcohol 95°	10 ounces

Preparation:

Bring the water to a boil, dissolve the sugar in it, remove from the heat immediately and let the syrup cool. Grind the oranges and macerate this pulp with the alcohol and the cooled syrup in an air-tight glass jar for two days, shaking well several times each day. Then, strain through a colander and filter paper into a dark-glass bottle and cork. Let it mature quietly for five months before serving. Makes about 22 ounces.

Orange, Dry
Secorange

A dry citrus liqueur made of fresh orange juice, with an alcoholic content about 40°. It has a full orange flavor and is refreshing served at almost any time of day.

Ingredients:

fresh orange juice	16 ounces
orange	sliced peel of one whole orange (only the orange part)
lemon	sliced peel of 2 whole lemons (only the yellow)
cloves	4 whole
cinnamon stick	½-inch piece
tangerine or tangelo	1 small, quartered
sugar	4 ounces
alcohol 95°	12 ounces

Preparation:

Combine the orange juice with all of the other ingredients in an air-tight glass jar and macerate for six months in a cool dark place, shaking the jar from time to time. At the end of the maceration period, strain through a colander and then through filter paper into a dark-glass bottle. Cork, seal with wax and let it mature quietly for five months before serving. Makes about 24 ounces.

Orange Flower
Fiorancio

Orange blossoms and rose petals form the base of this lovely and unusual liqueur. Its alcoholic content is about 40° and its taste is delicate and flowery.

Ingredients:

orange blossom	40 petals
domestic rose	20 petals
sugar	10 ounces
water	8 ounces
alcohol 95°	10 ounces

Preparation:

Macerate the orange blossom and rose petals with the alcohol in an air-tight glass jar for five days. Then, bring the water to a boil, dissolve the sugar in it, cool and add this syrup to the jar. Shake well and macerate for another five days. After this period, strain through a colander and filter paper into a dark-glass bottle. Cork, seal with wax and let it mature quietly for six months before serving. Makes about 20 ounces.

Orange, Sweet
Dulcorange

A sweet citrus liqueur made of fresh-squeezed
orange juice. With a relatively low alcoholic content
— only 20° — it is a perfect dessert liqueur.

Ingredients:

fresh orange juice	18 ounces
lemon	sliced peel of 3 whole lemons (only the yellow) and the juice of 1 whole lemon
caraway	a pinch of seeds
sugar	14 ounces
alcohol 95°	6 ounces

Preparation:

Strain the orange juice into an air-tight glass
jar with the lemon juice, lemon peel,
caraway, sugar and alcohol and macerate
for six months, shaking from time to time to
help mix the ingredients. After the
maceration period, strain through
cheesecloth and filter paper into a dark-
glass bottle. Cork, seal with wax, and set
aside in a cool place to mature quietly for
five months before serving. Makes about 25
ounces.

Orange Vermouth
Verange

Orange juice, dry vermouth and melissa combine to produce this soft, aromatic liqueur. It has an alcoholic content about 40° and a taste as appealing as its bouquet.

Ingredients:

oranges	3 medium juice oranges
cloves	4 whole
lemon	sliced peel of one whole lemon (only the yellow)
sugar	8 ounces
melissa	10 leaves
alcohol 95°	20 ounces
dry white vermouth	20 ounces

Preparation:

Cut the oranges with their peels into halves and macerate in an air-tight glass jar with the cloves, lemon peel, melissa, sugar and alcohol for one month. Then, add the vermouth, close the jar and let it stand for one more month, shaking the jar from time to time to help mix the ingredients. At the end of this maceration period, press through a colander, squeezing the juice out of the orange halves, and strain this liquid through filter paper into dark-glass bottles. Cork, seal with wax and let it mature quietly for seven months before serving. Makes about 48 ounces.

Oranges in Liqueur
Arance Sotto Spirito

Sweet mature oranges are steeped in liqueur
to create a robust digestive of about 45° alcohol with
a taste reminiscent of cointreau. The oranges
may be served separately and make a delightful dessert.

Ingredients:

oranges	5 medium navel oranges
cloves	3 whole
cinnamon stick	½-inch piece
sugar	16 ounces
alcohol 95°	24 ounces

Preparation:

Perforate the oranges with a fork in a number of places and place them in a large, air-tight glass jar. Add the rest of the ingredients, cover tightly and macerate for six months, shaking and turning once a week. At the end of this time, remove the oranges from the jar and strain the liqueur through filter paper. Wash the glass jar thoroughly and return the oranges and strained liqueur to it. Close and let it stand for two weeks before serving. The fruit is best served cut into quarters and sugared. Makes about 40 ounces.

Peach

Peschen

This fascinating and classic liqueur is made from the leaves of the peach tree. About 38° alcohol, it is particularly welcome served after a fine dinner.

Ingredients:

peach	70 leaves
lemon	sliced peel of ½ lemon (only the yellow)
sparkling white wine, semi-sweet	24 ounces
sugar	4 ounces
alcohol 95°	10 ounces

Preparation:

Place all of the ingredients in an air-tight glass jar and macerate for six weeks, shaking occasionally during this time. At the end of the maceration period, strain through a colander and through filter paper into a dark-glass bottle. Cork, seal with wax and let it mature quietly for nine months before serving. Makes about 34 ounces.

Pear
Perolo

A lovely liqueur made from sweet ripe pears faintly touched with apples and herbs. It has an alcoholic content of 40° and a taste that seems to suggest "autumn".

Ingredients:

pears, mature ripe	1 pound
apple thinly sliced peel of 2 apples	
cloves	2 whole
coriander	3 seeds
cinnamon stick	½-inch piece
nutmeg, grated	a pinch
sugar	10 ounces
alcohol 95°	12 ounces

Preparation:

Cut the pears into thin strips and place them in an air-tight glass jar along with the sugar, half of the alcohol, the apple peel, cloves, coriander, cinnamon and nutmeg. Macerate for two weeks, shaking the jar from time to time to help mix the ingredients. At the end of this period, strain through a colander, transfer the liquid to a dark-glass bottle and cork. Return the residue to the air-tight jar, add the rest of the alcohol, close and let stand for ten days, shaking from time to time. Strain through a colander and add this liquid to that in the dark-glass bottle. Mix well, close and let stand in a cool place for one week. Then, strain through filter paper into another dark-glass bottle, cork and seal with wax. Set it aside to mature quietly for six months before serving. Makes about 20 ounces.

Pineapple
Anasso

This delicately sweet liqueur has a base of ripe pineapple and an alcoholic content of about 40°. Its pleasant fruit bouquet gives only a hint of its rich fruit taste.

Ingredients:

pineapple pulp, fresh	1 pound
sugar	8 ounces
vanilla bean	½-inch piece
alcohol 95°	12 ounces

Preparation:

Peel the pineapple carefully and chop the flesh into small cubes. Place these in an airtight glass jar along with all the sugar, vanilla bean and alcohol and macerate for one week, shaking the jar twice a day to help mix the ingredients. At the end of the maceration period, strain through a colander and filter paper into a dark-glass bottle. Cork, seal with wax and let it mature quietly for eight months before serving. Makes about 22 ounces.

Pineapple Rum
Anarum

Sweet fresh pineapple steeped in rum makes for a dry and appealingly robust liqueur with an alcoholic content of 34°. It is also excellent served "on the rocks".

Ingredients:

pineapple pulp, fresh	½ pound
good quality rum	26 ounces

Preparation:

Peel the fresh ripe pineapple and chop the flesh into small pieces. Place these into an air-tight glass jar along with the rum and macerate for three weeks. Strain through a colander and filter paper into a dark-glass bottle and cork. Set aside to mature quietly for one or two months before serving. Makes about 28 ounces.

Plum, Sweet
Prusole

A liqueur made of sweet plums, with an alcoholic content about 38°. Sprinkled with a bit of sugar, the fruit can be used as a garnish for certain desserts.

Ingredients:

sweet plums	1¼ pounds
cloves	3 whole
lemon verbena	3 leaves
marsala wine	8 ounces
sugar	20 ounces
alcohol 95°	16 ounces

Preparation:

Place the whole plums, sugar, marsala wine and half of the alcohol into a clear air-tight glass jar. Close tightly and set in the sun for a few days, shaking from time to time until all of the sugar has dissolved. Then add the rest of the alcohol, cloves and lemon verbena. Reclose the jar and let it stand in a cool dark place for two months, shaking occasionally. After this maceration period, strain through cheesecloth and filter paper into a dark-glass bottle and cork. Let it mature quietly for two months before serving. Makes about 40 ounces.

Plum, Wild

Pruspino

This liqueur is made from wild or tart plums and has an alcoholic content about 41°. It has a pleasantly sharp taste and is best served after dinner.

Ingredients:

wild or tart plums	1 pound
sugar	10 ounces
alcohol 95°	16 ounces
cloves	5 whole
cinnamon stick	½-inch piece

Preparation:

Wash and dry the plums and spread them out on paper in the sun for one day. Then place them in a clear air-tight glass jar along with all of the other ingredients and set the jar in the sun for one week, shaking frequently to help the sugar dissolve. After this time, transfer the jar to a cool dark place for another six weeks. Strain through a colander and filter paper into a dark-glass bottle, cork and let it mature quietly for six months before serving. Makes about 24 ounces.

Plums in Liqueur
Prugne Sotto Spirito

Sweet prune plums steeped in liqueur make for an excellent digestive with an alcoholic content of about 38° and a taste reminiscent of slivovitz.

Ingredients:

sweet prune plums	1 pound
cloves	4 whole
cinnamon stick	½-inch piece
caraway	a pinch of seeds
sugar	8 ounces
alcohol 95°	12 ounces

Preparation:

Place the whole plums in an air-tight glass jar along with the cloves, cinnamon stick, caraway, sugar and alcohol and macerate for six months. Shake a few times during the first three months to help mix the ingredients. Strain off the spices before serving the liqueur. The plums may be sugared and served separately for dessert. Makes about 18 ounces.

Tangerine and Lemon Verbena Liqueur

Pomegranate
Pomgrane

A delightfully aromatic liqueur, about 42° alcohol,
made from the juice of pomegranates. It has an appealing
deep-red color and a superb, rich fruit taste.

Ingredients:

pomegranates	about 5 medium, or enough for 16 ounces of juice
caraway	1 teaspoon of seeds
hibiscus	1 tablespoon of petals
lemon	sliced peel of ¼ lemon (only the yellow)
sugar	6 ounces
alcohol 95°	12 ounces

Preparation:

Squeeze the pomegranates and strain out 16 ounces of juice. Pour the juice into an airtight glass jar along with the sugar, alcohol, caraway, hibiscus petals and lemon peel. Close tightly and macerate for one month, shaking from time to time to help mix the ingredients. After the maceration period, strain through cheesecloth and filter paper into a dark-glass bottle, cork and seal with wax. Set aside to mature quietly for five months before serving. Makes about 28 ounces.

Quince
Cotognolo

This unusual liqueur is made from the peel of ripe quince.
About 38° alcohol, it has a slightly bitter but
soothing taste and is particularly welcome after dinner.

Ingredients:

ripe quince	½ cup thinly sliced peel
sugar	10 ounces
brandy	13 ounces
alcohol 95°	6 ounces
water	6 ounces

Preparation:

Macerate the quince peel with the brandy and alcohol in an air-tight glass jar for 40 days in a cool dry place. Bring the water to a boil and dissolve the sugar in it. Cool and add this syrup to the jar. Close tightly, shake well and let it stand for one week. Then, strain through a colander and filter paper into a dark-glass bottle. Cork, seal with wax and set aside to mature quietly for six months before serving. Makes about 28 ounces.

Raspberries in Liqueur
Lamponi Sotto Spirito

Sweet ripe raspberries steeped in a lightly spiced liqueur
create a delicious after-dinner cordial, about
40° alcoholic content, with a lovely pale rose color.
The fruit may be served separately as a dessert.

Ingredients:

red raspberries	1 pound
alcohol 95°	10 ounces
cloves	2 whole
cinnamon stick	½-inch piece
lemon	sliced peel of ¼ lemon (only the yellow)
cherry, tart	15 leaves
sugar	4 ounces

Preparation:

Place all of the ingredients into an air-tight glass jar and macerate for six months. After the maceration period, the liqueur can be strained off and bottled to be served by itself. Sprinkled with a little sugar, the raspberries may be served for dessert over ice cream or cake. Makes about 24 ounces.

Raspberry
Lamponi

A liqueur with a base of red raspberries and an alcoholic
content about 38°. It has an inviting rose color,
a full fruit taste, and is delightful at almost any time.

Ingredients:

red raspberries	1 pound
cherry, tart	15 leaves
sugar	20 ounces
lemon	sliced peel of ½ lemon
	(only the yellow)
alcohol 95°	16 ounces

Preparation:

Place all the ingredients in a clear air-tight
glass jar and macerate in the sun for one
month, shaking frequently. Then, transfer
the jar to a cool dark place for another five
months. After the maceration period, strain
through a colander and through filter paper
into a dark-glass bottle and cork. Set aside
for one more month before serving. Makes
about 40 ounces.

Raspberry, Sweet
Lampocchero

This sweet liqueur made of fresh raspberries has an alcoholic content of only 14°. It can be served as an after-dinner cordial, used as a dessert syrup, and is particularly refreshing "on the rocks" with a splash of water.

Ingredients:

fresh raspberries	1 pound
sugar	16 ounces
lemon	sliced peel of ½ lemon (only the yellow)
cherry, tart	10 leaves
alcohol 95°	5 ounces

Preparation:

Place all of the ingredients in a clear air-tight glass jar and macerate in the sun for two months, shaking the jar frequently to help the sugar dissolve. Then, transfer the jar to a cool dark place and let it mature quietly for three more months. Strain through cheesecloth before serving. Makes about 18 ounces.

Rhubarb
Barbaro

An unusual liqueur with a base of fresh rhubarb and an alcoholic content about 33°. The slightly tart aftertaste of the fruit is surprising and pleasant. It may be served either as an aperitif or digestive.

Ingredients:

rhubarb	6 ounces of ground stalks
orange	sliced peel of ½ orange
artichoke	6 leaves
sugar	8 ounces
semi-dry white wine	34 ounces
alcohol 95°	8 ounces

Preparation:

Macerate the rhubarb, orange peel and artichoke leaves with the alcohol in an air-tight glass jar for five days. Then, dissolve the sugar in the wine and add this to the contents of the jar. Mix well and let it stand for another five days. At the end of this maceration period, strain through a colander and filter paper into a dark-glass bottle, cork and seal with wax. Set aside to mature quietly for two months before serving. Makes about 48 ounces.

Rose
Rosella

This sweet liqueur has a base of rose petals, an alcoholic content about 41°, and a bouquet and taste that are soft and flowery. It can be served for almost any occasion.

Ingredients:

domestic rose	40 petals
sugar	12 ounces
water	10 ounces
alcohol 95°	12 ounces

Preparation:

Mix the rose petals well with four ounces of the sugar, beating for a few minutes and adding a little of the alcohol. Pour the rose petal mixture into an air-tight glass jar with the rest of the alcohol. Close tightly and let it stand for ten days, shaking a few times to help mix the ingredients. Then, bring the water to a boil and dissolve the rest of the sugar in it. Cool completely and add this syrup to the contents of the jar. Close again, shake well, and let it stand for one week. At the end of this period, strain through a colander and through cheesecloth into a dark-glass bottle. Cork, seal with wax and set aside to mature quietly for two to four months before serving. Makes about 24 ounces.

Rose and English Walnut

Rosnoce

This aromatic liqueur is made with a base of rose petals and English walnuts. With an alcoholic content of only 18°, it is particularly good as an aperitif.

Ingredients:

domestic rose	30 petals
English walnuts	5 whole
cloves	5 whole
cinnamon stick	½-inch piece
lemon	sliced peel of 1 whole lemon (only the yellow)
lemon verbena	4 leaves
semi-sweet white wine	20 ounces
alcohol 95°	4 ounces

Preparation:

This original recipe for this liqueur calls for green or unripe English walnuts and utilizes the entire nut, including the outer hull which can be cut through easily when it is green. If only dried English walnuts are available — the kind sold commercially — use just the nut meats and not the shells. The taste will be somewhat different, but still quite good. Cut the walnuts into quarters and place them in an air-tight glass jar with all the other ingredients to macerate for 40 days, shaking a few times during the maceration period. Then, strain through a colander and filter paper into a dark-glass bottle. Cork, seal with wax and let it mature quietly for eight months before serving. Makes about 24 ounces.

Sage
Salviolo

A semi-dry liqueur with a base of sage, alcoholic content
about 39°. It has excellent digestive qualities
and a taste and bouquet that are delightfully aromatic.

Ingredients:

sage	25 leaves
thyme	a pinch
lime	1 whole, quartered
sweet sparkling white wine	16 ounces
sugar	6 ounces
alcohol 95°	10 ounces

Preparation:

Cut the lime into quarters and place it in an air-tight glass jar with all the other ingredients. Macerate for one month, shaking once a day during the maceration period. Then, strain through a colander and filter paper into a dark-glass bottle, cork and seal with wax. Let it rest quietly for eight months before serving. Makes about 26 ounces.

Sage, Sweet
Salvietta

This is a sweet liqueur with a base of sage and an alcoholic content about 37°. It has a full rich taste, fine digestive qualities and is welcome at any time of the day.

Ingredients:

sage	33 leaves
basil	2 leaves
cloves	3 whole
lemon	sliced peel of 3 whole lemons (only the yellow)
dry white wine	24 ounces
sugar	24 ounces
alcohol 95°	20 ounces

Preparation:

Macerate all of the ingredients in a large air-tight glass jar for six weeks, shaking a few times to help the sugar dissolve. Then, strain through cheesecloth into a dark-glass bottle, cork and seal with wax. Set aside to mature quietly for six months before serving. Makes about 48 ounces.

Strawberry
Fragolo

A sweet fruit liqueur made with a base of fresh ripe strawberries. About 40° alcohol, it is best served after dinner or with dessert. The strawberries may also be served as a dessert garnish for ice cream or cake.

Ingredients:

strawberries	¾ pound
vanilla	a pinch of crushed bean
sugar	14 ounces
water	4 ounces
alcohol 95°	14 ounces

Preparation:

Wash and dry the strawberries quickly so they don't become saturated with water and place them in an air-tight glass jar with all of the other ingredients. Macerate for four weeks, turning very delicately once a day. At the end of the maceration period, strain through a colander and several thicknesses of cheesecloth into a dark-glass bottle. Cork, seal with wax and let it mature quietly for seven months before serving. The strawberries may be stored in a closed jar in the refrigerator for use as described above. Makes about 26 ounces.

Tangerine and Lemon Verbena

Luigiolo

A delightfully aromatic dry liqueur with a base of tangerines and lemon verbena. It has an alcoholic content about 42° and is best served as a digestive.

Ingredients:

lemon verbena	25 leaves
tangerines	3 medium, quartered
cloves	3 whole
cinnamon stick	a pinch
thyme	a pinch
caraway seeds	a pinch
sugar	4 ounces
dry white wine	20 ounces
alcohol 95°	8 ounces

Preparation:

Combine all of the ingredients in an air-tight glass jar and macerate for five weeks, shaking very delicately from time to time. At the end of the maceration period, strain through a colander and filter paper into a dark-glass bottle, cork and seal with wax. Let it mature quietly for seven months before serving. Makes about 25 ounces.

Tangerine Brandy
Brandytai

This dry liqueur has a base of tangerines and brandy and an alcoholic content about 40°. It is an excellent digestive and is especially welcome after a fine dinner.

Ingredients:

tangerines	4 medium, quartered
brandy	26 ounces

Preparation:

Macerate the tangerines with the brandy in an air-tight glass jar for 40 days. At the end of this period, strain through a colander and filter paper into a dark-glass bottle, cork and seal with wax. Let it rest quietly for eight months before serving. Makes about 26 ounces.

Tangerine, Dry
Mandotai Secco

Tangerines lightly spiced with cinnamon and cloves are the base for this dry liqueur. It has an alcoholic content of 40°, a superb aroma and a robust taste.

Ingredients:

tangerines	3 medium, quartered
water	10 ounces
sugar	4 ounces
cloves	4 whole
cinnamon stick	a pinch
alcohol 95°	12 ounces

Preparation:

Place all of the ingredients in an air-tight glass jar and macerate for five months, shaking from time to time. Then, strain through a colander and filter paper into a dark-glass bottle. (The residue in the colander may be used to make Tangerine Vermouth.) Cork, seal with wax and let it mature quietly for six months before serving. Makes about 24 ounces.

Tangerine, Sweet

Mandolai Dolce

This sweet liqueur has a base of tangerines and
an alcoholic content about 35°. It has a distinctive,
pleasant bouquet and a smooth, mellow taste
that makes it suitable to be served at any time of day.

Ingredients:

tangerines	4 medium, quartered
lemon	sliced peel of 1 whole lemon (only the yellow)
cloves	2 whole
sugar	12 ounces
alcohol 95°	14 ounces
dry white vermouth	8 ounces

Preparation:

Place all of the ingredients in an air-tight glass jar to macerate for six months, shaking very delicately from time to time. Then, strain through cheesecloth into a dark-glass bottle. (The residue may be used to make Tangerine Vermouth.) Cork, seal with wax and let it mature quietly for six months before serving. Makes about 26 ounces.

Tangerine Vermouth

Vertai

This liqueur has a base of tangerines and dry vermouth. Its low alcoholic content, only 17°, and appealingly sharp taste make it particularly welcome as an aperitif.

Ingredients:

strained residue from the preparation of Dry or Sweet Tangerine liqueur
dry white vermouth   32 ounces

Preparation:

Place the tangerine residue into an air-tight glass jar, add the vermouth, close tightly and let it stand for six months. At the end of this period, strain through a colander and filter paper into a dark-glass bottle, cork and let it mature quietly for two months before serving. Makes about 32 ounces.

Tarragon
Genepi

An unusual herb liqueur made with a base of tarragon.
Its alcoholic content is about 42° and its
taste and bouquet are pleasantly sweet and aromatic.

Ingredients:

tarragon	25 leaves fresh or
	1 tablespoon dry
sugar	12 ounces
water	12 ounces
alcohol 95°	10 ounces

Preparation:

Combine the tarragon with the alcohol in an air-tight glass jar, macerate for four weeks, then strain through filter paper. Bring the water to a boil and dissolve the sugar in it. Cool and add this syrup to the strained tarragon-alcohol liqueur. Mix well, funnel into a dark-glass bottle, cork and seal with wax. Let it mature quietly for eight months before serving. Makes about 24 ounces.

Tart Green Grape
Uviolo

A fruit liqueur with a base of tart green grapes.
Its low alcoholic content, about 25°, and exquisite grape
taste make it a welcome cordial at any time of day.

Ingredients:

grapes, green and tart	about 1¼ pounds or enough for 16 ounces of juice
cloves	4 whole
coriander	1 tablespoon seeds
cinnamon stick	½-inch piece
brandy	16 ounces
sugar	4 ounces
alcohol 95°	4 ounces

Preparation:

Macerate the alcohol, cloves, cinnamon and coriander in an air-tight glass jar for two weeks. Then, stirring constantly, heat the grapes over very low heat until the skins pop open. Pour them into a colander lined with fine cheesecloth and press out 16 ounces of juice. Dissolve the sugar in the warm juice, cool and add to the contents of the jar. Mix well but delicately and let the jar stand for another five weeks. Then, strain through a colander and filter paper into a dark-glass bottle. Cork, seal with wax and let it mature quietly for nine months before serving. Makes about 36 ounces.

Tart Green Grape Vermouth
Zuvio

This sweet liqueur combines tart green grape liqueur
and vermouth. With its low alcoholic content, about 18°,
it is excellent as an aperitif and can also be
served as a dessert sauce over fruits, puddings and tarts.

Ingredients:

tart green grape liqueur from the preceding recipe	16 ounces
lemon verbena	3 leaves
dry white vermouth	16 ounces
alcohol 95°	4 ounces
sugar	12 ounces

Preparation:

Stir the sugar into the grape liqueur, bring it to a boil and simmer for two to four minutes, keeping the heat low. Cool and pour this syrup into an air-tight glass jar along with the vermouth, alcohol and lemon verbena. Close tightly, mix well and let it macerate for three to four months, shaking from time to time. Then, strain through cheesecloth into dark-glass bottles and cork. The liqueur may be served immediately but the bouquet is vastly improved if it rests a few months longer. Makes about 38 ounces.

Ten Herbs
Erba 10

Ten familiar herbs combine to produce a fine tonic-digestive liqueur with an appealing semi-sweet taste and an alcoholic content of 36°.

Ingredients:

lemon	6 leaves
melissa	5 leaves
mint	10 leaves
bay leaves	3 whole
camomile	a pinch of blossoms
juniper	6 berries
rosemary	a good-sized pinch
cloves	6 whole
cinnamon stick	½-inch piece
dandelion root	a pinch
alcohol 95°	12 ounces
sugar	12 ounces
dry white vermouth	12 ounces

Preparation:

Macerate the alcohol and vermouth with all of the other ingredients except the sugar in an air-tight glass jar for 15 days. Then, strain through filter paper into a dark-glass bottle into which the sugar has already been funneled. Cork, seal with wax and shake once a day for one month. Let it rest for five more months and strain through filter paper into another dark-glass bottle. Cork, seal with wax and set aside to mature quietly three months longer before serving. Makes about 26 ounces.

Thirty Herbs
Trenterbe

A classic herb liqueur — centuries old — with
a base of 30 different herbs and an alcoholic content
of 40°. It has a distinctive taste and
bouquet as well as excellent digestive qualities.

Ingredients:

bay leaves	2 whole
anise	a pinch of seeds
wormwood	a pinch
camomile	4 blossoms
fuller's teasel	½ root, chopped
thistle	½ root, chopped
carrot seeds	a pinch
caraway seeds	a pinch
lemon verbena	4 leaves
lime	sliced peel of ¼ lime (only the green)
cloves	4 whole
chicory	½ root, chopped
coriander	4 seeds
gentian	a pinch of root
juniper	4 berries
hibiscus	1 tablespoon blossoms, chopped
melissa	4 leaves
peppermint	4 leaves
pennyroyal	4 leaves
artichoke	4 leaves
tangerine	1 medium, quartered
licorice root	a pinch
green English walnut or shelled dry walnut	1 whole, quartered
rose	10 petals
rhubarb	6-inch stalk, chopped
orris root	a pinch
oregano	a pinch
calamus	a pinch
tea	1 teaspoon
thyme	a pinch
sugar	8 ounces
dry white wine	10 ounces
alcohol 95°	10 ounces

Preparation:

Macerate all of the herbs with the alcohol in
an air-tight glass jar for ten days. Then, dissolve the sugar in the wine and add this
syrup to the jar. Mix well, close tightly and
let it stand for another 20 days. After this
period, strain through filter paper into a
dark-glass bottle, cork and seal with wax.
Let it mature quietly for seven months
before serving. Makes about 24 ounces.

Twelve Bitters
Amaro 12

This pleasantly sharp dry liqueur has a base of various herbs. Its alcoholic content is relatively low, about 30°; its tonic and digestive qualities are superb.

Ingredients:

melissa	5 leaves
sage	5 leaves
rosemary	10 leaves
centaury	1 blossom
juniper	15 berries
cloves	5 whole
cinnamon stick	½-inch piece
orris root	a pinch
calamus	a pinch
gentian	a pinch of root
thistle	a pinch of chopped root
bay leaves	2 whole
sugar	6 ounces
dry white vermouth	26 ounces
alcohol 95°	8 ounces

Preparation:

Macerate all of the herbs with the alcohol in an air-tight glass jar for five days. Strain the liquor into a dark-glass bottle and return the residue to the air-tight jar. Dissolve the sugar in the vermouth and macerate with the residue in the jar for another five days. Strain and add to the liquor in the dark-glass bottle. Mix well and let it stand for one day. Then, strain through filter paper into a clean dark-glass bottle, cork and seal with wax. Set aside to mature quietly for eight months before serving. Makes about 34 ounces.

A Calendar of Liqueurs

Following is a list of the best months in which to make various liqueurs — the times when the ingredients required are most readily available:

January

Almond; Bitter Orange; Coconut; Coffee; Cream Marsala; Dry Orange; Eggnog; Lemon and Orange; Milk and Cherries; Orange and Lemon; Orange Vermouth; Oranges in Liqueur; Pineapple; Pineapple Rum; Rhubarb; Sweet Orange.

February

Almond; Bitter Orange; Coffee; Cream Marsala; Dry Orange; Dry Tangerine; Eggnog; Lemon and Orange; Milk and Cherries; Orange and Lemon; Orange Vermouth; Oranges in Liqueur; Pineapple; Pineapple Rum; Rhubarb; Sweet Orange; Sweet Tangerine; Tangerine and Lemon Verbena; Tangerine Brandy; Tangerine Vermouth.

March

Almond; Coconut; Coffee; Cream Marsala; Dry Tangerine; Eggnog; Milk and Cherries; Pineapple; Pineapple Rum; Rhubarb; Sweet Tangerine; Tangerine and Lemon Verbena; Tangerine Brandy; Tangerine Vermouth.

April

Almond; Artichoke; Artichoke Brandy; Banana; Coconut; Coffee; Cream Marsala; Eggnog; Loquat or Yellow Plum; Milk and Cherries; Pineapple; Pineapple Rum; Sweet Loquat or Yellow Plum.

May

Almond; Artichoke; Artichoke Brandy; Banana; Coconut; Coffee; Cream Marsala; Eggnog; Loquat or Yellow Plum; Milk and Cherries; Sage; Sweet Loquat or Yellow Plum; Sweet Sage.

June

Almond; Apple-Tea; Apricot; Banana; Black Cherry; Camomile; Caraway; Cherry; Cherry Leaf; Coconut; Coffee; Cream Marsala; Dry English Walnut; Eggnog; English Walnut; English Walnut Brandy; English Walnut Vermouth; Green Tomato; Hibiscus and Camomile; Jujubes in Liqueur; Melissa; Milk and Cherries; Mixed Mint; Morello or Tart Cherry; Mulberry; Orange Flower; Peach; Pear; Rose; Rose and English Walnut; Sage; Semi-Dry Cherry Leaf; Strawberry; Sweet Cherry; Sweet Sage; Wild Carnation.

July

Absinthe; Almond; Apple-Tea; Apricot; Black Cherry; Black Currant; Blackberries in Liqueur; Blackberry Brandy; Camomile; Caraway; Cherry; Cherry Leaf; Coconut; Coffee; Cream Marsala; Dry Lemon Verbena; Eggnog; Elderberries, Huckleberries or Bilberries in Liqueur; Elderberry, Huckleberry or Bilberry; Four Fruits; Fourteen Herbs; Gooseberry; Green Tomato; Herbs and Brandy; Hibiscus and Camomile; Jujubes in Liqueur; Melissa; Milk and Cherries; Mixed Mint; Morello or Tart Cherry; Orange Flower; Peach; Pear; Plums in Liqueur; Raspberries in Liqueur; Raspberry; Rose; Sage; Semi-Dry Cherry Leaf; Strawberry; Sweet Cherry; Sweet Elderberry, Huckleberry or Bilberry; Sweet Plum; Sweet Raspberry; Sweet Sage; Tarragon; Ten Herbs; Wild Carnation.

August

Absinthe; Almond; Aromatic Bitters; Black Currant; Blackberries in Liqueur; Blackberry Brandy; Caraway; Coconut; Coffee; Cream Marsala; Eggnog; Elderberries, Huckleberries and Bilberries in Liqueur;

Elderberry, Huckleberry and Bilberry; Four Fruits; Fourteen Herbs; Gooseberry; Hibiscus and Camomile; Jujubes in Liqueur; Lemon Verbena; Melissa; Milk and Cherries; Mixed Mint; Pear; Plums in Liqueur; Raspberries in Liqueur; Raspberry; Sage; Strawberry; Sweet Elderberry, Huckleberry and Bilberry; Sweet Plum; Sweet Raspberry; Sweet Sage; Tangerine and Lemon Verbena; Tarragon; Thirty Herbs; Twelve Bitters; Wild Carnation.

September

Absinthe; Almond; Arbutus in Liqueur; Bay Leaf; Blackberries in Liqueur; Blackberry Brandy; Coconut; Coffee; Cream Marsala; Dry Lemon Verbena; Eggnog; Lemon Verbena; Milk and Cherries; Mountain Ash; Tart Green Grape; Tart Green Grape Vermouth; Thirty Herbs; Twelve Bitters; Wild Plum.

October

Almond; Apple; Apples in Liqueur; Arbutus in Liqueur; Coconut; Coffee; Cream Marsala; Eggnog; Juniper; Milk and Cherries; Mountain Ash; Pear; Pomegranate; Quince; Tart Green Grape; Tart Green Grape Vermouth; Wild Plum.

November

Almond; Apple; Apples in Liqueur; Arbutus in Liqueur; Bitter Orange; Coconut; Coffee; Cream Marsala; Eggnog; Juniper; Milk and Cherries; Orange and Pear; Pear; Pineapple; Pineapple Rum; Pomegranate; Quince; Tart Green Grape; Tart Green Grape Vermouth.

December

Almond; Apple; Apples in Liqueur; Arbutus in Liqueur; Bitter Orange; Coconut; Coffee; Cream Marsala; Dry Orange; Eggnog; Lemon and Orange; Milk and Cherries; Orange and Lemon; Orange Vermouth; Oranges in Liqueur; Pineapple; Pineapple Rum; Sweet Orange.

Index of Liqueur Recipes

Absinthe	14	Coconut	42
Almond	15	Coffee	43
Apple	16	Cream Marsala	44
Apple-Tea	19		
Apples in Liqueur	20	Eggnog	45
Apricot	21	Elderberries, Huckleberries	
Arbutus in Liqueur	22	or Bilberries in Liqueur	46
Aromatic Bitters	23	Elderberry, Huckleberry	
Artichoke	24	or Bilberry	47
Artichoke and Brandy	25	Elderberry, Huckleberry	
		or Bilberry, Sweet	48
Banana	26	English Walnut	49
Bay Leaf	27	English Walnut Brandy	50
Blackberries in Liqueur	28	English Walnut, Dry	51
Blackberry Brandy	29	English Walnut Vermouth	52
Black Currant	30		
		Four Fruits	55
Camomile	31	Fourteen Herbs	56
Caraway	32		
Carnation, Wild	33	Gooseberry	57
Cherry	34	Green Tomato	58
Cherry, Black	37		
Cherry Leaf	38	Herbs and Brandy	59
Cherry Leaf, Semi-Dry	39	Hibiscus and Camomile	60
Cherry, Morello or Tart	40		
Cherry, Sweet	41	Jujubes in Liqueur	61

Juniper	62	Plum, Wild	88
		Plums in Liqueur	91
Lemon and Orange	63	Pomegranate	92
Lemon Verbena	64		
Lemon Verbena, Dry	65	Quince	93
Loquat or Yellow Plum	66		
Loquat or Yellow Plum, Sweet	67	Raspberries in Liqueur	94
		Raspberry	95
Melissa	68	Raspberry, Sweet	96
Milk and Cherries	69	Rhubarb	97
Mixed Mint	70	Rose	98
European Mountain Ash	73	Rose and English Walnut	99
Mulberry	74		
		Sage	100
Orange and Lemon	75	Sage, Sweet	101
Orange and Pear	76	Strawberry	102
Orange, Bitter	77		
Orange, Dry	78	Tangerine and Lemon Verbena	103
Orange Flower	79	Tangerine Brandy	104
Orange, Sweet	80	Tangerine, Dry	105
Orange Vermouth	81	Tangerine, Sweet	106
Oranges in Liqueur	82	Tangerine Vermouth	109
		Tarragon	110
Peach	83	Tart Green Grape	111
Pear	84	Tart Green Grape Vermouth	112
Pineapple	85	Ten Herbs	113
Pineapple Rum	86	Thirty Herbs	114
Plum, Sweet	87	Twelve Bitters	115